Vera Wilsie Fl...
1988-89 Nu... mini-grant

From Grass to Butter

DISCARD

Vera Wilsie Library
Newaygo, Michigan

From Grass to Butter

Ali Mitgutsch

 Carolrhoda Books, Inc., Minneapolis

First published in the United States of America 1981 by
Carolrhoda Books, Inc. All English language rights reserved.

Original edition © 1972 by Sellier Verlag GmbH, Eching bei München,
West Germany, under the title VOM GRAS ZUR BUTTER.
Revised English text © 1981 by Carolrhoda Books, Inc.
Illustrations © 1972 by Sellier Verlag GmbH.

Manufactured in the United States of America

LIBRARY OF CONGRESS CATALOGING IN PUBLICATION DATA

Mitgutsch, Ali.
From grass to butter.

(A Carolrhoda start to finish book)
Edition for 1972 published under title: Vom Gras zur Butter.
SUMMARY: Briefly explains how grass is used by cows to produce milk which is made into butter.

1. Dairying—Juvenile literature. 2. Milk—Juvenile literature. 3. Butter—Juvenile literature. [1. Dairying. 2. Milk. 3. Butter] I. Title.

SF239.5.M5513   1981   637   80-28588
ISBN 0-87614-156-4

2 3 4 5 6 7 8 9 10 86 85 84 83 82

From Grass to Butter

Here is a cow eating fresh, green grass.
The grass will help the cow produce milk.
Milk is used to make butter.
Cows' milk is stored in their **udders**.
The udder is the baggy sack that hangs down in front of the cow's hind legs.

The farmer milks his cows twice a day:
once in the morning and once at night.
The milking is done by a machine
that is hooked up to the cows' udders.
Before this machine was invented,
farmers milked their cows by hand.

The full milk cans are picked up
from all the farms in the area
and taken to the **dairy**.
If the milk is not picked up right after milking,
it must be stored in a refrigerator.
Otherwise it will spoil and turn sour.

When the milk gets to the dairy,
it is put into a huge container.
Then it is heated and quickly cooled.
This is called **pasteurizing** (PASS-chuh-rize-ing).
Pasteurizing kills any disease-causing germs
that might be in the milk.
Some of the milk will now become drinking milk,
and some will be used to make other dairy products.

The milk that will be used to make butter
is put into a machine
called a **centrifuge** (SEHN-trih-fewj).
The centrifuge spins around very fast.
It separates the skim milk
from the thick sweet cream.
The skim milk and the cream
flow into separate containers.

The sweet cream is now put into a butter machine.
In this machine, the cream is stirred for a long time.
First the cream becomes foamy.
Then small solid flakes form.
Soon they join together into lumps of butter.
The sour liquid that is left after the butter forms
is called buttermilk.

When the butter comes out of the machine,
it is packaged and taken to stores.
You can find many other products made from milk
at your local grocery store.
Cheese, yogurt, ice cream, and whipping cream
all come from milk.

Butter is just one of the many products
that is made from milk.
Can you think of others?

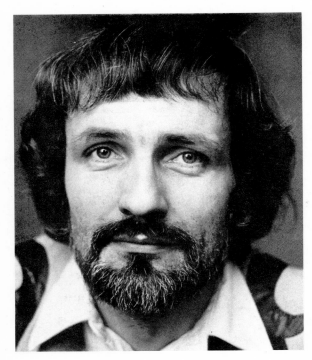

Ali
Mitgutsch